Bigotry

And Greed

Can destroy all

People, families, communities, nations.

Knowledge requires patience.

Honesty demands

Apology.

PK
2016

America Cries:
"I'm Sorry!"

US Apologies for
Japanese Internment,
Hawaiian Annexation,
Slavery,
Treatment of Native Americans,
and Chinese Exclusion

A Collection of Essays

William M. Kirtley, Lem Londos Railsback
Patricia M. Kirtley, William R. Curtis
Terry L. Lovelace

First Edition

America Cries:

"I'm Sorry!"

A Collection of Essays

Dedication

*We dedicate this book
to all who have the courage to tender
apologies
and to the recipients
who have the wisdom and integrity to accept
them.*

Acknowledgements

To Jack Holland, friend and student of Lem, who prepared this work for publication.

To Estin Kiger, Tai Chi teacher and artist, who designed the front and back cover.

To Esther Kwan at the Chinese Cultural Center in San Francisco, who first mentioned America's Five Apologies on her city walking tour.

To Pat Kirtley, our editor, for harmonizing the work of five authors.

To the Fabulous Five for dedication, cooperation, and determination.

Thank you!

America Cries: "I'm Sorry!"

**US Apologies for
Japanese Internment,
Hawaiian Annexation,
Slavery,
Treatment of Native Americans,
and Chinese Exclusion**

A Collection of Essays

by

William M. Kirtley
Lem Londos Railsback
Patricia M. Kirtley
William R. Curtis
Terry L. Lovelace

Contents

Introduction

Apologies are potent, symbolic, and thaumaturgical acts. There are three types of apologies: individual, intra-state, and inter-national. Ordinary people, Presidents, and Popes all make apologies. A sincere apology must include saying you are sorry and meaning it. An apology accepted normalizes social relations. This process generates public debate about national histories and reconciliation. It strengthens those who apologize. Reparations have restorative value. Fate condemns those who refuse to apologize, out of ignorance or hubris, to an endless cycle of accusation and recrimination.

The five apologies discussed in this collection of essays are from the President and/or Congress of the United States to injured parties for actions motivated by cupidity and racism: Japanese internment and relocation of the Aleuts, slavery, the overthrow of the Hawaiian kingdom, treatment of Native Americans, and Chinese exclusion.

Apology for Japanese Internment
by
William M. Kirtley

On 7 December 1941, fourteen year-old Edwin Nakasone looked up from breakfast and watched fifteen Japanese aircraft headed for Pearl Harbor. A few days later, authorities jailed his father who had recently returned from a trip to Japan. They questioned his father, held him overnight, and returned him to his family (Nakasone Interview). The government initially detained 1800 Japanese Americans in Hawaii and 5500 on the mainland. The detainees were community leaders, Buddhist priests, newspaper editors, and language teachers. The government never accused any of the detainees of a crime. The thesis of this essay is the U.S. government interned Japanese in Hawaii and on the mainland because of fear, racism, and greed.

On 19 February 1942, President Franklin D. Roosevelt signed an Executive Order authorizing military commanders to exclude persons deemed a threat to national security. The order did not use the word internment. It mentioned the government would provide food, shelter, and transportation (original document reproduced in Brooks, p. 169). Military commanders ordered 120,000 Japanese Americans on the West coast to register, sell their property, put their possessions in storage, and report to assembly areas. Two-thirds of them were US citizens and half of the 120,00 were children. A heart rending graphic novel *Gaijin: American prisoner of war* by Matt Faulkner (2014) described the process of exclusion and internment of a teenager with a Japanese father and Caucasian mother.

President Roosevelt established the War Relocation Authority on 18 March 1942. This government agency built camps in isolated and remote areas and provided for their administration. They located two camps in the states of California, Arkansas, and Arizona and still others in Idaho, Wyoming, Utah, and Colorado. Each camp housed approximately 10,000 Japanese Americans. The government provided medical care, schools, and common dining, bathing, and toilet facilities. Camp authorities allowed residents to work outside the camp as agricultural laborers (Okubo, p. 12).

Soldiers guarded the perimeter of the camp, not to protect the inhabitants, but to keep them in. Roy Saigo, now President of Southern Oregon University, recalled the barbed wire. He remembered "the guards would shoot you if you tried to leave" (cited in Perrier, 2005, p. 210). He recalled his parents' worries. "They didn't know if we might be gassed or shot" (cited in Perrier, 2005, p. 210).

The War Relocation Authority used control of the media to frame their actions as benign. Jim Marshall (1942) in an article for *Collier's Weekly,* "The Problem People," justified internment on the grounds "there is some human instinct that keeps the races apart" (p. 34). A War department newsreel (1943) stated the Army carried out internment, "As a real democracy should, with consideration for the people involved" (War department newsreel: Japanese relocation, 1943).

In contrast, the images of three photographers, Ansel Adams, Dorthea Lang, and Toyo Miyatake conveyed a sense of pride, heartbreak, and desolation that censorship could not diminish. The War Relocation Authority did not allow internees to possess cameras. However, Miyatake smuggled a camera in a specially built box into Camp Manzanar, California.

Japanese Americans displayed a diversity of opinions as befits a democratic community. Members of the Japanese American Citizens League, an organization that lobbied for citizenship rights before the war, urged its members to go peaceably into the camps. In contrast, Gordon Hirabayashi, Fred Korematsu, and, Minoru Yasui refused internment. The US government arrested and imprisoned them.

George Takei the author, director, activist, and former internee is best known for his role as Sulu, the navigator of the *Starship Enterprise*. A 2016 Broadway musical, *Allegiance,* isbased on his family's real life camp experiences. Takei expressed regret for his arrogance in chiding his father for peaceably entering the internment camps (Suzuki 2008). He vividly remembered the moment when he rebuked his father."Daddy, you led us like sheep to slaughter into the internment camp…. My father looked at me and said, 'Well, maybe you are right.' My father got up, went to his bedroom and closed the door" (Takei, 2015, November 20). Takei's pride prevented him from apologizing, even though he knew his father dedicated every moment of his life to restoring their family to normalcy. Takei failed to voice an apology before his father died. The last scene in *Allegiance* provides him an opportunity for expiation and atonement.

Conflict continued inside the camps. Sam Hohri, editor of *Free Press,* the newspaper at Camp Manzanar, suggested compliance with authorities in the interest of national defense. Japanese Americans educated in Japan, advocated resistance. In the winter of 1943, the War Relocation Authority asked internees to complete a loyalty questionnaire. They labeled those who desired deportation, remained loyal to the Emperor, or refused to volunteer for duty in the Armed Forces, "disloyal" (15%). They sent these so-called "no-no boys" to a detention camp at Tule Lake, California (Niiya, 2014, p. 1).

The respondents to this questionnaire suffered practical and ethical dilemmas. Mine Okubo in her starkly illustrated graphic novel *Citizen 13660* (1946) noted those born in Japan could not, by law, become naturalized citizens. If they renounced their Japanese citizenship, they would become stateless persons (p. 165). The governing authority of the camps, the War Relocation Authority, asked those born in the United States, and therefore citizens, to volunteer for military service for a country that imprisoned their parents and siblings.

The government closed the camps in 1945. The internees returned to their communities and attempted to resume their lives. Many encountered distrust and discrimination. Issei (1st generation) leaders made it clear they did not wish to stir up "old bad feelings" (Daniels, "Relocation," 1999, p. 183). Sentiment in the Japanese community shifted, as one generation gave way to the next. Congress established the Commission on Wartime Relocation and

Internment of Civilians in 1980 to investigate Japanese-American requests for an apology and reparations.

This Commission heard testimony and issued a two-part report in 1983. The first part called for an apology to Japanese Americans interned by the government, pardons for those who refused internment, action by the government to deal with losses incurred by the internees, establishment of an educational foundation, and reparations of $20,000 paid to each Japanese American interned (Daniels, "Redress," 1999, p. 189).

The second part of the Congressional Commission's report concerned the involuntary evacuation of 881 Aleuts from the Aleutian archipelago. The Imperial Japanese Army invaded the islands of Attu and Kiska in 1942 as a diversion for their attack on Midway Island. They captured ninety American citizens, villagers and weather observers, and sent them to prison camps in Japan. As a result, the U.S. Army decided to forcibly remove indigenous peoples, even those with as little as one-eighth Native American blood, from all the Pribilof and Aleutian Islands.

The US Army relocated these indigenous peoples in squalid relocation camps in Southwest Alaska. Camps included an abandoned gold mine and a deserted fish cannery provided one toilet for 200 people located on the tidal flats (Cueva, p.1). Local Native Americans taught the newcomers survival skills in this new and strange environment. Many of the Aleuts had never seen trees (Cueva, p. 1). One in ten Aleuts died under these sordid conditions (Kashima, and Williams,

p. 1).

The U.S. soldiers and sailors who occupied the home villages of the Aleuts nearly obliterated the unique culture of these indigenous people. Members of the military smashed precious icons, defiling the religious heritage gained from Russian Orthodox missionaries. They looted and vandalized Aleut homes. The Commission on Wartime Relocation and Internment of Civilians recommended Congress pay compensation, considering the deplorable treatment and conditions the Aleuts endured.

Grayce Uyehara, a social worker from Philadelphia, spearheaded the lobbying effort. Uyehara feared veterans groups might object to giving $1.25 billion to Japanese American internees. She urged her supporters to spread the message of the sacrifice and heroism two Japanese American units, the 442nd Regimental Combat Team and the 100th Infantry Battalion of the Hawaii National Guard. This forestalled the development of any real opposition. Members of Congress voted without fear of retribution by their constituents, a so-called "free vote" (Hatamiya, 1999, p. 192).

Congresspersons of Japanese descent, led by decorated war veteran Senator Matsunaga (D-HI), talked to every member of Congress. Rep. Barney Frank (D-MA) shepherded the legislation through various committees. In 1988, Congress passed the Civil Liberties Act, which wrote into law the recommendations of the Congressional Committee. President George H. W. Bush issued a formal apology on 7 December 1991. President Bill Clinton apologized on 1 October 1993 (See Appendix). Some members of Congress disagreed. Daniel Lundgren (R-CA) believed reparations were unnecessary. He feared the Act would fuel the demands of African Americans and Native Americans for apologies and reparations. Rep. Norman Mineta (D-CA) replied, "At issue here is wholesale violation, based on race, of those whose legal principles we were fighting to defend" (cited in Daniels, "Redress," 1999,p. 161).

The government of the United States yielded to racism, greed, and hysteria. It ordered many of its own citizens into internment camps without due process of law. Japanese Americans worked with interest groups and elected officials to gain redress. The US government interned the parents and grandparents of Ellen Somekawa. She termed the apology, "a huge thing" (Gammage, 2003, p. 2). She declared it was an exciting opportunity to highlight an important chapter in American history. Japanese Americans like Somekawa gained the sincere and full apology they sought, and established a paradigm for other groups to follow, a model never fully replicated.

Resources

Brooks, R. (Ed). (1999). *When sorry isn't enough.* New York: New York University.

Bush, G. (1988, August 10). Letter from President George Bush to Japanese Internees. Retrieved from http://www.learner.org/courses/amerhistory.

Clinton, B. (1993, October 1). Apology letter from President Bill Clinton. Retrieved from http://www.pbs.org/childofcamp/history/clinton.html.

Cueva, C. (1998). America's territory, The Aleut evacuation: A grave injustice. Retrieved from http://www.akhistorycourse.org/articles/article.php?artiD=215.

Daniels, R. (1999). Redress achieved, 1983-1990. In Brooks, R. (Ed.) *When sorry isn't enough.*

Daniels, R. (1999). Relocation, redress, and the report. In Brooks, R. (Ed.) *When sorry isn't enough.*

Faulkner, M. (2014). *Gaijin: American prisoner of war.* New York: Hyperion Books.

Gammage, J. (2013, November 15). Honoring a leader in a fight for Japanese American redress. *Philadelphia Inquirer,* p. A02.

Hatamiya, L. (1999). Institutions and interest groups. In Brooks, R. (Ed.) *When sorry isn't enough.*

Kashima, T. and Williams, M. (2004, February 19) WW II an American tragedy. A guest opinion. *Seattle Times:* p. 1.

Niiya, B. (2014). No-no boys. *Densho Encyclopedia.* Retrieved from http://encyclopeid.densho.org.

Okubo, M. (1946) *Citizen 13660.* Seattle: University of Washington Press.

Perrier, R. (2005). *A sense of honor.* Minneapolis (MN): Archie Publications.

Public Law 100-383. (1988, Aug. 10). Signed by President Ronald Reagan authorizing compensation for Japanese and Aleuts. Retrieved fromwww.internmentarchives.com/showdoc.php?docid=00172&...

Roosevelt, F. (1942, February 19). [document] reproduced in Brooks, R. (Ed.) *When sorry isn't enough.* p. 169.

Suzuki, J. (Writer and Director) (2008). *Toyo's camera.* [DVD]. Produced by UTB and Film Voice. Retrieved from www.toyoscamera.com.

Takei, G. 2015, November 20). Takei's

heartbreaking words to his father. Major missed keypoints of history. Retrieved from www.youtube.com/watch?v=0g8yf1zZ941.

Taylor, S. (1999). The internment of Americans of Japanese ancestry. In Brooks, R.   (Ed.) *When sorry isn't enough.*

Marshall, J. (1942, August 15). The problem people. *Collier's Magazine*, p. 30.

Nakasone, E. (2014, December 8). E-mail interview.

Tavuchis, N. (1991) *Mea culpa.* Stanford: Stanford University Press.

War department newsreel: Japanese relocation (1943). YouTube www.youtubecom.

A. Appendix for Japanese-Americans

A.1. Excerpt from Public Law 100-383 -
Public Law 100-383. (1988, Aug. 10). Signed by President Ronald Reagan authorizing compensation for Japanese and Aleuts. Retrieved from www.internmentarchives.cop.php?docid=00172&

An Act To implement recommendations of the Commission on Wartime Relocation and Internment of Civilians. Be it enacted by the Senate and House of Representatives of the United States of America in Congress assembled,

Section 1. The purposes of this Act are to—
(1) acknowledge the fundamental injustice of the evacuation, relocation, and removal of United States citizens and permanent resident aliens of Japanese ancestry during World War II;

(2) apologize on behalf of the people of the United States for the evacuation, relocation, and internment of such citizens and permanent resident aliens;

(3) provide for a public education fund to finance efforts to inform the public about the internment of such individuals so as to prevent the recurrence of any similar event;

(4) make restitution to those individuals of Japanese ancestry who were interned;

(5) make restitution to Aleut residents of the Pribilof Islands and the Aleutian Isleuids west of

Unimak Island, in settlement of United States obligations in equity and at law, for—

(A) injustices suffered and unreasonable hardships endured while those Aleut residents were under United States control during World War II;

(B) personal property taken or destroyed by United States forces during World War II;

(C) community property, including community church property, taken or destroyed by United States forces during World War II; and

(D) traditional village lands on Attu Island not rehabilitated after World War II for Aleut occupation or other productive use;

(6) discourage the occurrence of similar injustices and violations of civil liberties in the future; and

(7) make more credible and sincere any declaration of concern by the United States over violations of human rights committed by other nations.

SEC. 2. Statement of the Congress

(a) With regard to individuals of Japanese ancestry —The Congress recognizes that, as described by the Commission on War-time Relocation and Internment of Civilians, a grave injustice was done to both citizens and permanent resident aliens of Japanese ancestry by the evacuation, relocation, and internment of civilians during World War II. As the Commission documents, these actions were carried out without adequate security reasons and without any acts of espionage or sabotage documented by the Commission, and were motivated largely by racial prejudice, wartime hysteria, and a failure of political leadership. The excluded individuals of Japanese ancestry suffered enormous damages, both material and intangible, and there were incalculable losses in education and job training, all of which resulted in significant human suffering for which appropriate compensation has not been made. For these fundamental violations of the basic civil liberties and constitutional rights of these individuals of Japanese ancestry, the Congress apologizes on behalf of the Nation.

(b) With respect to the Aleuts. The Congress recognizes that, as described by the Commission on Wartime Relocation and Internment of Civilians, the Aleut civilian residents of the Pribilof Islands and the Aleutian Islands west of Unimak Island were relocated during World War II to temporary camps in isolated regions of southeast Alaska where they remained, under United States control and in the care of the United States, until long after any potential danger to their home villages had passed. The United States failed to provide reasonable care for the Aleuts, and this resulted in widespread illness, disease, and death among the residents of the camps; and the United States further failed to protect Aleut personal and community property while such property was in its possession or under its control. The United States has not compensated the Aleuts adequately for the conversion or destruction of personal property, and the conversion or destruction of community property caused by the United States military occupation of Aleut villages during World War II.

There is no remedy for injustices suffered by the Aleuts during World War II except an Act of Congress providing appropriate compensation for those losses which are attributable to the conduct of United States forces and other officials and employees of the United States.

A.2. Bush Apology - Letter from President George Herbert Walker Bush (1988, August 10). to Japanese Internees. Retrieved from http://www.learner.org/courses/amerhistory/int eractives/sources/E7/e1/sources/5496.php.

The White House
Washington
August 10, 1988

A monetary sum and words alone cannot restore lost years or erase painful memories; neither can they fully convey our Nation's resolve to rectify injustice and uphold the rights of individuals. We can never fully right the wrongs of the past. But we can take a clear stand for justice and recognize that serious injustices were done to Japanese Americans during World War II.

In enacting a law calling for restitution and offering a sincere apology, your fellow Americans have, in a very real sense, renewed their traditional commitment to the ideals of freedom, equality, and justice. You and your family have our best wishes for the future.

Sincerely,
(signed)
George Bush

A.3. Clinton Apology - Clinton, B. (1993, October 1). Apology letter from President Bill Clinton. Retrieved from http://www.pbs.org/childofcamp/history/clinton.html

The White House
Washington
October 1, 1993

Over fifty years ago, the United States Government unjustly interned, evacuated, or relocated you and many other Japanese Americans. Today, on behalf of your fellow Americans, I offer a sincere apology to you for the actions that unfairly denied Japanese Americans and their families fundamental liberties during World War II.

In passing the Civil Liberties Act of 1988, we acknowledged the wrongs of the past and offered redress to those who endured such grave injustice. In retrospect, we understand that the nation's actions were rooted deeply in racial prejudice, wartime hysteria, and a lack of political leadership. We must learn from the past and dedicate ourselves as a nation to renewing the spirit of equality and our love of freedom. Together we can guarantee a future with liberty and justice for all. You and your families have my best wishes for the future.

Sincerely,
(signed)
Bill Clinton

"Apology" for Illegal Overthrow of the Hawaiian Monarchy (Hawaiian Rape)
By
Lem Londos Railsback

The theft of Hawaii was the perfect example of "the white man's burden" a special "philosophy" that reflected the erection of the British Empire around the world, but especially in India and China and parts of Africa and, later, the erection of the American Empire.

The Brewing of a Giant Argument

In 1859—after his "round the world" trip aboard the Beagle vessel, Charles Darwin published his amazing *On the Origin of Species*.("Charles Darwin," p. 1.) From reading Darwin, Herbert Spencer coined the phrase, "survival of the fittest." ("Survival of the Fittest," p. 1.) What Darwin was delineating, as eventually deciphered by other scientists with high I.Q.'s, was his notion of "natural selection." That selection by nature was determined by how well an organism could reproduce and keep the most offspring alive amidst all the various challenges of its environment. Historically, however, the phrase was initially and usually incorrectly interpreted to "justify" all sorts of misdeeds, particularly racism and greed—e.g., "Manifest Destiny." This famous phrase was unfortunately interpreted widely as referring to "nature's law" which dictated that only the toughest, strongest, and, even, meanest and continually fighting creatures survived. Using the particular philosophy of "the white man's burden"—even before Kipling's famous poem was written--the British Empire was established and administered around the world. (An old saying was that "The sun never sets on the British Empire." After all, "Great Britain" became the strongest naval force in the world. The Empire administered conquered/"bought" lands around the globe through their administrative, naval, commercial, and military might.) In the Boxer Rebellion in China, the imperialist countries Great Britain, France, Germany, Italy, Japan, Russia, Austria-Hungary, and the United States defeated the Boxers, a religious society of patriotic Chinese who were attempting to throwout the foreigners' influences for commercialism, imperialism, drug-use, and Christian missionary proselytization. Upon victory, each conquering nation established a "sphere of influence." In each sphere, the ruling power encouraged the growing of opium for which they paid very little to the Chinese agricultural workers or "coolies" who farmed the product. Then, the ruling power would process the opium into heroin, alkaloid morphine, opiates codeine, and other synthetic opiods and sell their products back home and internationally at extremely high levels of profit. Whenever the ruling power sold the same products to the coolies themselves, the prices remained extremely inflated.

Within a short time in the United States, the notion of "manifest destiny" had taken root. That notion held that since the colonists had "whupped the Brits" and won their independence, put down a lot of Indians and taken their native lands, installed a system of slavery of Irish and Negroes and others, and then began settling the West, then, truly, the Christian God Almighty must have meant for them to do so. And since those western settlers were white, then the Christian God Almighty must have meant for the white Americans to do all that: therefore, they had the obligation—the "White Man's Burden"-- to settle the land from east to west and from south to north to Canada and to direct the lives and save the souls of the reds, blacks, yellows, browns, and sun-darks. A clear difference arose, then. in the minds of these burden-carrying whites, between themselves—the *destined*—and all of those native populations—the heathens or the *undestined*. Meanwhile, the enormous bargain on the Louisiana Purchase, the gain of much of Mexico's land after the War of 1848, and other adventures favored the white *destines*. Even after the American Civil War had "ended" slavery, the states in the South passed laws in the 1890's to maintain the divinely *destined* dividing walls between the *destined* and the *undestined*. For the United States of that time to fully and precisely carry its God-determined obligation, the international version of the "White Man's Burden" pushed further beyond the Pacific coastline so that by the beginning of the twentieth century, the U.S. "controlled much of Alaska, Cuba, the Philippines, Puerto Rico, Hawaii, and Guam." *(United States History, Chapter 3. Populism and Imperialism, 1890—1900*, p. 2.) Of course, those Christian God Almighty-chosen whites brought the blessings of liberty, economic opportunities for individuals, representative government, and other blessings to all of those conquered peoples, even without the conquered peoples' consent and with the loss of their cultures, their religions, their former ways of life, and for many, their very lives.

In February 1899, the British poet and novelist Rudyard Kipling penned his "The White Man's Burden: The United States and the Philippine Islands." (To read a copy of the complete poem, see "Modern History Sourcebook: Rudyard Kipling, The White Man's Burden, 1899," pp. 1-2.) On its surface, the poem was "emblematic both of Eurocentric racism and of Western aspirations to improve and industrialize the developing world." ("The White Man's Burden," p. 1.) Publication of the famous and inflammatory poem "coincided with the beginning of the Philippine-American War and U.S. Senate ratification of the treaty that placed Puerto Rico, Guam, Cuba, and the Philippines under American control." ("'The White Man's Burden': Kipling's Hymn to U.S. Imperialism," *History Matters: The U.S. Survey Course on the Web*, p. 1.) On the surface, Kipling's poem appears to promote the white man's burden/obligation to "save" and "civilize" and "Christianize" the natives of the conquered lands. However, a closer reading may reveal that Kipling was actually warning against imperialism in light of the various costs to the conquering nation and its treasured values. Of course, the majority of the early readers in the United States interpreted, as per their preferences for imperialism and Christianizing, the surface meaning of Kipling's poem.

A Particular Target for the Burdened White Man

A small group of islands that we today call "Hawaii" sits at about the middle of the Pacific Ocean between North America and Asia. In the eighth century, the small group of islands were

34

inhibited by visitors from the Polynesian Islands to the southwest. According to oral tradition, the priest Pa'ao brought the native Tahitian naturalist religion with many deities to Hawaii. Spanish explorers visited the islands in the late sixteenth century, but journeyed on to the Philippines, their favored target. Then, on January 18, 1778, Captain James Cook visited and named the islands "Sandwich Islands" in honor of the then-First Lord of the Admiralty John Montagu, 4th Earl of Sandwich. ("Hawaiian Islands," p. 1.)

New Visitors with Their Accompaniments

In the new British protectorate, a local chief named Kamehameha secured British guns and artillery to conquer/absorb all of the islands and rule as king. Along with British guns came the diseases of measles, flu, whooping cough, cholera, and VD. Also accompanying the British were alcohol, tobacco, fleas, mosquitos, and other foreigners. About one-half of the natives died in the 1803 cholera epidemic. In 1819, the king died. By the 1820's, the islands had become a port-of-call for international traders and whalers. Foreign diplomats, businessmen, and others arrived and began renting properties from the king. They persuaded the monarchy to develop large tracts for growing sandalwood, a very profitable export at the time. The change from the native small farming economy to a modern agricultural money economy, wherein the former small farmers became lowly wage-earners, began to enrich the foreigners and belittle the former small farmers. Their traditional Hawaiian religion and customs were belittled. In 1835, sugar cane plantations began to supplant the sandalwood tracts. ("Robert Louis Stevenson and the Kingdom of

Hawaii," Mick Arellano (2006). *A Traveler's History of Hawaii*. Agile Guidebooks, pp. 1-2.)

New Serious and Godly Visitors
with New and Godly Serious Ideas

In 1820, the American Board of Commissioners for Foreign Missions sent its first group of missionaries to the islands. Over the next several decades, the Board sent eleven more groups. Zealous missionaries from the Anglican, Catholic, Church of Latter Day Saints, Congregational, Presbyterian, Russian Orthodox, and other denominations worked to save the "heathen Hawaiians." Toward the same goal, Tahitian protestant and Hawaiian protestant missionaries worked. In time, tension among the congregations and the native religion prompted King Kamehameha III to issue the Edict of Toleration whereby the missionaries and the natives could practice their preferred respective religions. The new constitution of 1840 provided religious liberty for all. Some sects grew large and powerful. "By 1865, the Church of Latter Day Saints had purchased a 6,000-acre plantation in La'ie." ("History of the Polynesian Cultural Center and Mormonism in Hawaii," p. 1.).

Stealing the Kingdom of Hawaii
for The White God Almighty's Kingdom

Throughout the nineteenth century, the different Hawaiian kings were challenged by the wealthy landowners and their associates. Pushing for a written constitution modeled after that of the U.S., the *destines* seriously challenged the monarchy: the new 1840 law of the land gave "common Hawaiians political power for the first time in their history." Later, the constitution of 1852 seriously limited even further the powers of the king. Although King Kamehameha V's constitution of 1864 did restore some of the monarch's powers, it imposed new property-ownership and educational requirements on voters, severely diminishing the political power of common Hawaiians. It also cancelled the house of representatives. The sugar growers grew in power so much that they supported David Kalakaua as the new king and gained the Reciprocity Treaty of 1876 whereby Hawaiian sugar could be sold in the U.S. without paying import duties.

Born in 1836, Kalakaua studied at the Royal School, began studying law at sixteen, and by age twenty had achieved the rank of major on the staff of King Kamehameha IV. He joined the Young Hawaiians whose motto was "Hawaii for Hawaiians." In 1874, he was elected to the throne. For the planters, he travelled to the U.S.—the first Hawaiian king to do so—and secured the Reciprocity Treaty of 1876, which enormously favored the planters' wealth and political strength. For his native citizens, he worked to restore the commoners' culture, religion, and political power. He circumnavigated the world in 1871 and, again, in 1887. To resist the imposing imperialism of the U.S. and other nations, the king visited many countries and met with many of their leaders. He proposed to the Japanese Emperor the formation of an Asiatic Federation among Hawaii, Japan, and other nations. He invited Japan to send workers to the fields of Hawaii: thousands came. He constructed a great home for himself and his bride and friends: the innovative home had electricity and indoor plumbing. His friend Thomas Edison visited and shot the very first movies of Hawaiians. His friend

Robert Louis Stevenson visited numerous times and sided with Kalakaua's attempts to bring back the native culture as per his slogan "Hawaii for Hawaiians," to "grant universal suffrage to women and the poor," to bring back native "hula and chants, surfing and indigenous handicrafts," and to grow strong political ties with powerful nations, especially Japan, around the globe. (VagoKamitio, "ROBERT LOUIS STEVENSON—WRITING VAGABOND," *Vagobond*, p. 3.) Such actions were taken by the disgruntled d*estineds* to constitute threats to their political and economic powers. And, of course, they were correct. (VagoKamitio, "ROYAL VAGABOND—KING DAVIDE KALAKAUA—THE MERRIE MONARCH,:*Vagobond*, pp. 1-8. Finally settling in Samoa, Stevenson took the Samoans' side of the political argument with the wealthy *destined* planters.)

In 1888, the *destineds*formed an armed Honolulu Rifle Company. That HRC was led by Lorrin A. Thurston, a *destined* "grandson of two of the first Christian missionaries to Hawai'i, whose grandfather Asa Thurston and grandmother LudyGoodale had arrived with the first ABCFM group. Lorrin A. Thurston's HRC forced Kalakaua to sign the "Bayonet Constitution," so-called for obvious reasons. ("Lorrin A. Thurston," *Wikipedia*, pp. 1-3.) This new constitution, once again, bolstered the political and economic might of the *destineds* and severely limited the eco-political and cultural might of the native *undestineds*. After sailing to California in late 1890 to seek medical treatment, King Lalakaua died in January 1891. His sister Liliuokalani ascended to the throne.

One of the most *destineddestineds*, John L. Stevens—journalist, author, politician, minister, newspaper publisher, and a founder of the Republican Party in Maine--went on record several times to preach manifest destiny. His former newspaper publisher partner James G. Blaine continued to work within/for the Republican Party until he was nominated as a presidential candidate in 1876 and, again, in 1880. For Blaine's support, President Garfield named him as his Secretary of State. Blaine was a public and determined promoter of the manifest destiny doctrine. ("James G. Blaine," pp. 7-12.) Stevens persuaded his old *destined* partner to appoint him as "Minister Plenipotentiary and Envoy Extraordinary" to Hawaii. After arriving at his new post, Stevens requested that the USS Boston, a warship, "be stationed indefinitely in Honolulu harbor." ("John L. Stevens," pp. 1-5.)

Queen Liliuokalani attempted to promulgate a new constitution which would restore the powers of the monarchy and restore voting rights to the commoners. Such actions angered the *destineds*, again led by Lorrin A. Thurston, who formed the Annexation Club.

On January 14, 1893, Minister Stevens met with two other men concerned about American territorial interests in the Pacific. That night, Stevens and American—Hawaiian businessmen Sanford B. Dole and Lorrin Thurston met to hatch 'an audacious plot to overthrow Hawaii's Queen and bring her country into the United States. (*Ibid.*, p. 3.)

Thurston's Annexation Club quickly morphed into the Committee of Safety and began preparing documents for a new government. On January 16, 1893, Envoy Stevens, claiming that Americans and their properties were in danger, summoned 162 Marines and sailors from the USS Boston. But, instead of providing protection for Americans and their properties, the well-armed marines and sailors surrounded Hawaiian government buildings and royal residences. In light of the overwhelming odds against her and In order to avoid bloodshed of any of her Hawaiian subjects, Queen Lili'uokalani ordered her armed forces to stand down and then abdicated. Immediately, the Honolulu Rifles took over the government buildings and set up a provisional government. The *destined* Sanford B. Dole, whose parents Daniel Dole and Emily Hoyt Ballard had arrived with the ninth ABCFM group, was installed as president. With the militarily superior U.S. marines and sailors and economically superior wealthy planters, Dole began his dictatorial rule of the Islands and of their peoples, outright casualties of the White Man's Burden. ("Queen Liliuokalani and the American Take-over of Hawaii," EDB, The University of Texas, p. 3. For additional insights, see, also, "Sanford Ballard Dole," *Encyclopedia Britannica*, p. 1.)Then, they imprisoned the queen and seized 1.75 million acres of royal land.

("Eugene Tyler Chamberlain, The Hawaiian Situation: The Invasion of Hawaii," *Digital History*, p. 1. For further documentations and particular insights, see, also, the following reports."Jan. 17, 1893: Hawaiian Monarchy Overthrown by America-Backed Businessmen, *The New York Times*.For a succinct yet amazing versions, view "Overthrow of the Kingdom of

Hawaii," *Wikipedia*, and the "Americans overthrow Hawaiian monarchy, *History.com*/. For involvement of our top "leaders" in the grand theft of Hawaii, view "U.S. Government in the Overthrow," *hawaiialive.org*/. To glimpse the wide opposition to the annexation, view "Annexation of Hawaii," *United States Imperialism*.) As the *coup d'etat*was completed, Stevens established a protectorate and sent emissaries to Washington, D.C., to push for annexation. President Harrison sent his request for annexation on February 16 to congress. The newly elected President Cleveland cancelled the annexation process and sent a commissioner to the islands to investigate. The investigator recommended that the new protectorate be withdrawn. Stevens resigned. On July 17, 1893, the Blount Report declared that Stevens had acted inappropriately. For his reply, Stevens, in the true nature and spirit of a true *destined,* declared that "the queen was immoral, and so needed to be dethroned." (John L. Stevens, *op. cit.*, p. 4.)Later, in 1898, a different congress and a different president—McKinney—annexed Hawaii and appointed the *destined* Sanford B. Dole as territorial governor.

During the remainder of her life—i.e., until 1917, the queen wrote her autobiography. She also penned the famous international parting song "Aloha Oe" ("Farewell To Thee"). On August 21, 1959, Hawaii was granted statehood. Much later, on the basis of Queen Lili'uokalani's autobiography and many other supporting documents, "In 1993, on the one-hundred-year anniversary of the coup, President Clinton signed a bill into law formally apologizing to Hawaii for the illegal invasion by the United States." ("Queen Liliuokalani and the American Take-over of Hawaii," *op. cit.*, p. 3.)

Resources

Kamitio, Vago, "ROBERT LOUIS STEVENSON—
WRITING VAGABOND," *Vagobond*.
Retrieved from
http://www.vagobond.comn/robert-louis-
stevenson-writing-vagabond/.

Kamitio, Vago, "ROYAL VAGABOND—KING
DAVIDE KALAKAUA—THE
MERRIEMONARCH,:*Vagobond*.
Retrieved from
http://www.vagobond.com/royal-
vagabond-king-david-kalakaua-the-merrie-
monarch/.

"Americans overthrow Hawaiian monarchy,
History.com. Retrieved from
http://www.history.com/this-day-in-
history/americans-overthrow-hawaiian-
monarchy.

"Annexation of Hawaii," *United States
Imperialism*. Retrieved from
http://unitedstatesimperialism.wordpress.
com/about/.

"Charles Darwin," E*NCYCLOPEDIA
BRITANNICA. Retrieved from*
http://www.britannica.com/EBchecked/to
pic/151902/Charles-Darwin.

"Eugene Tyler Chamberlain, The Hawaiian
Situation: The Invasion of Hawaii," *Digital
History*. Retrieved from

http://www.digitalhistory.uh.edu./disp_te
xtbook.cfm?smtlD=3&psid=4050.

"History of the Polynesian Cultural Center and
Mormonism in Hawaii," *The Polynesian
Culture Center and Mormonism in
Hawaii*. Retrieved from
http://ghhawaii.about.com/od/history//a/
pcc_history.htm.

"James G. Blaine," *Wikipedia*. Retrieved from
http://en.wikipedia.org/wiki/James_G_Bl
aine.

"Jan. 17, 1893: Hawaiian Monarchy Overthrown
by America-Backed Businessmen, *The New
York Times*. Retrieved from
http://learning.blogs.nytimes.com/2012/0
1/17/jan-17-1893-hawaiian-monarchy-
overthrown-by-american-backed-
businessmen/?_php=true&_type=blogs.

"John L. Stevens," *Wikipedia*. Retrieved from
http://en.wikipedia.org/wiki/John_L_Ste
vens.

"Lorrin A. Thurston," *Wikipedia*. Retrieved from
http://en.wikipedia.org/wiki/Lorrin_A_T
hurston.

"Modern History Sourcebook: Rudyard Kipling,
The White Man's Burden, 1899,"
*FORDHAM UNIVERSITY: THE JESUIT
UNIVERSITY OF NEWYORK*. Retrieved
from

https://legacy.fordham.edu/halsall/mod/K
ipling.asp.

"Overthrow of the Kingdom of Hawaii,"
    Wikipedia. Retrieved from
    http://en.wikipedia.org/wiki/Overthrow_o
    f_the_kingdom_of_hawaii

"Queen Liliuokalani and the American Take-over
    of Hawaii," *EDB, The University of Texas.
    Retrieved
    from*http://www.edb.utexas.edu/faculty/s
    alinas/students/student_sites/Fall2005/h
    awaii

"Robert Louis Stevenson and the Kingdom of
    Hawaii," Mick Arellano (2006). *A
    Traveler's History of Hawaii*. Agile
    Guidebooks. Retrieved from
    http://www.agilegidebooks.com/guidestoh
    istory/hawaii.

"Sanford Ballard Dole," *Encyclopedia Britannica*.
    Retrieved from
    http://www.britannica.colm/EBchecked/t
    opic/.168157/SanfordBallard-Dole.

"Survival of the Fittest," *Wikipedia*. Retrieved
    from
    http://en.wikipedia.org/wiki/Survival_of_
    the_fittest.

"The White Man's Burden," *Wikipedia. Retrieved
    from* https://en.wikipeduia.org/wiki/The
    White_Man%27s_Burden.

"'The White Man's Burden': Kipling's Hymn to U.S. Imperialism," *History Matters: The U.S. Survey Course on the Web. Retrieved from*http://historymatters.gmu.edu/d/5478/.

United States History, Chapter 3. Populism and Imperialism, 1890—1900. Retrieved from *http://2012books.lardbucket.org/books/united-states-history-volume-2/s06-populism-and-imperiallism-1890-.html.*

"U.S. Government in the Overthrow," *hawaiialive.org.* Retrieved from http://www.hawaiialive.org/topics/php?sub=Overthrow+and=Contemorary+Issues&Subtopic=50

B. Appendix for Hawaii

B.1. Joint Resolution 19 apologizing for the overthrow of the Kingdom of Hawaii.
United States Public Law 103-150. (1993, November 23). 103d Congress. Retrieved from http://www.hawaii-nation.org/publawall.html.

To acknowledge the 100th anniversary of the January 17, 1893 overthrow of the Kingdom of Hawaii, and to offer an apology to Native Hawaiians on behalf of the United States for the overthrow of the Kingdom of Hawaii.

Whereas, prior to the arrival of the first Europeans in 1778, the Native Hawaiian people lived in a highly organized, self-sufficient, subsistent social system based on communal land tenure with a sophisticated language, culture, and religion;

Whereas, a unified monarchical government of the Hawaiian Islands was established in 1810 under Kamehameha I, the first King of Hawaii;

Whereas, from 1826 until 1893, the United States recognized the independence of the Kingdom of Hawaii, extended full and complete diplomatic recognition to the Hawaiian Government, and entered into treaties and conventions with the Hawaiian monarchs to govern commerce and navigation in 1826, 1842, 1849, 1875, and 1887;

Whereas, the Congregational Church (now known as the United Church of Christ), through its American Board of Commissioners for Foreign Missions, sponsored and sent more than 100 missionaries to the Kingdom of Hawaii between 1820 and 1850;

Whereas, on January 14, 1893, John L. Stevens (hereafter referred to in this Resolution as the "United States Minister"), the United States Minister assigned to the sovereign and independent Kingdom of Hawaii conspired with a small group of non-Hawaiian residents of the Kingdom of Hawaii, including citizens of the United States, to overthrow the indigenous and lawful Government of Hawaii;

Whereas, in pursuance of the conspiracy to overthrow the Government of Hawaii, the United States Minister and the naval representatives of the United States caused armed naval forces of the United States to invade the sovereign Hawaiian nation on January 16, 1893, and to position themselves near the Hawaiian Government buildings and the Iolani Palace to intimidate Queen Liliuokalani and her Government;

Whereas, on the afternoon of January 17,1893, a Committee of Safety that represented the American and European sugar planters, descendants of missionaries, and financiers deposed the Hawaiian monarchy and proclaimed the establishment of a Provisional Government;

Whereas, the United States Minister thereupon extended diplomatic recognition to the Provisional Government that was formed by the conspirators without the consent of the Native Hawaiian people or the lawful Government of Hawaii and in violation of treaties between the two nations and of international law;

Whereas, soon thereafter, when informed of the risk of bloodshed with resistance, Queen Liliuokalani issued the following statement yielding her authority to the United States

Government rather than to the Provisional Government:

"I, Liliuokalani, by the Grace of God and under the Constitution of the Hawaiian Kingdom, Queen, do hereby solemnly protest against any and all acts done against myself and the Constitutional Government of the Hawaiian Kingdom by certain persons claiming to have established a Provisional Government of and for this Kingdom.
"That I yield to the superior force of the United States of America whose Minister Plenipotentiary, His Excellency John L. Stevens, has caused United States troops to be landed a [sic] Honolulu and declared that he would support the Provisional Government. "Now to avoid any collision of armed forces, and perhaps the loss of life, I do this under protest and impelled by said force yield my authority until such time as the Government of the United States shall, upon facts being presented to it, undo the action of its representatives and reinstate me in the authority which I claim as the Constitutional Sovereign of the Hawaiian Islands." Done at Honolulu this 17th day of January, A.D. 1893.

Whereas, without the active support and intervention by the United States diplomatic and military representatives, the insurrection against the Government of Queen Liliuokalani would have failed for lack of popular support and insufficient arms;
Whereas, on February 1, 1893, the United States Minister raised the American flag and proclaimed Hawaii to be a protectorate of the United States;

Whereas, the report of a Presidentially established investigation conducted by former Congressman James Blount into the events surrounding the insurrection and overthrow of January 17, 1893, concluded that the United States diplomatic and military representatives had abused their authority and were responsible for the change in government;

Whereas, as a result of this investigation, the United States Minister to Hawaii was recalled from his diplomatic post and the military commander of the United States armed forces stationed in Hawaii was disciplined and forced to resign his commission;

Whereas, in a message to Congress on December 18, 1893, President Grover Cleveland reported fully and accurately on the illegal acts of the conspirators, described such acts as an "act of war, committed with the participation of a diplomatic representative of the United States and without authority of Congress", and acknowledged that by such acts the government of a peaceful and friendly people was overthrown;

Whereas, President Cleveland further concluded that a "substantial wrong has thus been done which a due regard for our national character as well as the rights of the injured people requires we should endeavor to repair" and called for the restoration of the Hawaiian monarchy;

Whereas, the Provisional Government protested President Cleveland's call for the restoration of the monarchy and continued to hold state power and pursue annexation to the United States;

Whereas, the Provisional Government

successfully lobbied the Committee on Foreign Relations of the Senate (hereafter referred to in this Resolution as the "Committee") to conduct a new investigation into the events surrounding the overthrow of the monarchy;

Whereas, the Committee and its chairman, Senator John Morgan, conducted hearings in Washington, D.C., from December 27,1893, through February 26, 1894, in which members of the Provisional Government justified and condoned the actions of the United States Minister and recommended annexation of Hawaii;

Whereas, although the Provisional Government was able to obscure the role of the United States in the illegal overthrow of the Hawaiian monarchy, it was unable to rally the support from two-thirds of the Senate needed to ratify a treaty of annexation;

Whereas, on July 4, 1894, the Provisional Government declared itself to be the Republic of Hawaii;

Whereas, on January 24, 1895, while imprisoned in Iolani Palace, Queen Liliuokalani was forced by representatives of the Republic of Hawaii to officially abdicate her throne;

Whereas, in the 1896 United States Presidential election, William McKinley replaced Grover Cleveland;

Whereas, on July 7, 1898, as a consequence of the Spanish-American War, President McKinley signed the Newlands Joint Resolution that provided for the annexation of Hawaii;

Whereas, through the Newlands Resolution, the self-declared Republic of Hawaii ceded sovereignty over the Hawaiian Islands to the United States;

Whereas, the Republic of Hawaii also ceded 1,800,000 acres of crown, government and public lands of the Kingdom of Hawaii, without the consent of or compensation to the Native Hawaiian people of Hawaii or their sovereign government;

Whereas, the Congress, through the Newlands Resolution, ratified the cession, annexed Hawaii as part of the United States, and vested title to the lands in Hawaii in the United States;

Whereas, the Newlands Resolution also specified that treaties existing between Hawaii and foreign nations were to immediately cease and be replaced by United States treaties with such nations;

Whereas, the Newlands Resolution effected the transaction between the Republic of Hawaii and the United States Government;

Whereas, the indigenous Hawaiian people never directly relinquished their claims to their inherent sovereignty as a people or over their national lands to the United States, either through their monarchy or through a plebiscite or referendum;

Whereas, on April 30, 1900, President McKinley signed the Organic Act that provided a government for the territory of Hawaii and defined the political structure and powers of the newly established Territorial Government and its relationship to the United States;

Whereas, on August 21,1959, Hawaii became the 50th State of the United States;

Whereas, the health and well-being of the

Native Hawaiian people is intrinsically tied to their deep feelings and attachment to the land;

Whereas, the long-range economic and social changes in Hawaii over the nineteenth and early twentieth centuries have been devastating to the population and to the health and well-being of the Hawaiian people;

Whereas, the Native Hawaiian people are determined to preserve, develop and transmit to future generations their ancestral territory, and their cultural identity in accordance with their own spiritual and traditional beliefs, customs, practices, language, and social institutions;

Whereas, in order to promote racial harmony and cultural understanding, the Legislature of the State of Hawaii has determined that the year 1993, should serve Hawaii as a year of special reflection on the rights and dignities of the Native Hawaiians in the Hawaiian and the American societies;

Whereas, the Eighteenth General Synod of the United Church of Christ in recognition of the denomination's historical complicity in the illegal overthrow of the Kingdom of Hawaii in 1893 directed the Office of the President of the United Church of Christ to offer a public apology to the Native Hawaiian people and to initiate the process of reconciliation between the United Church of Christ and the Native Hawaiians; and

Whereas, it is proper and timely for the Congress on the occasion of the impending one hundredth anniversary of the event, to acknowledge the historic significance of the illegal overthrow of the Kingdom of Hawaii, to express its deep regret to the Native Hawaiian people, and to support the reconciliation efforts of the State of

Hawaii and the United Church of Christ with Native Hawaiians;

Now, therefore, be it

Resolved by the Senate and House of Representatives of the United States of America in Congress assembled,

Section 1. Acknowledgment and Apology

The Congress -

(1) on the occasion of the 100th anniversary of the illegal overthrow of the Kingdom of Hawaii on January 17, 1893, acknowledges the historical significance of this event which resulted in the suppression of the inherent sovereignty of the Native Hawaiian people;

(2) recognizes and commends efforts of reconciliation initiated by the State of Hawaii and the United Church of Christ with Native Hawaiians;

(3) apologizes to Native Hawaiians on behalf of the people of the United States for the overthrow of the Kingdom of Hawaii on January 17, 1893 with the participation of agents and citizens of the United States, and the deprivation of the rights of Native Hawaiians to self-determination;

(4) expresses its commitment to acknowledge the ramifications of the overthrow of the Kingdom of Hawaii, in order to provide a proper foundation for reconciliation between the United States and the Native Hawaiian people; and

(5) urges the President of the United States to also acknowledge the ramifications of the overthrow of the Kingdom of Hawaii and to support reconciliation efforts between the United States and the Native Hawaiian people.

SEC. 2. Definitions.
As used in this Joint Resolution, the term "Native Hawaiians" means any individual who is a descendent of the aboriginal people who, prior to 1778, occupied and exercised sovereignty in the area that now constitutes the State of Hawaii.

SEC. 3. Disclaimer.
Nothing in this Joint Resolution is intended to serve as a settlement of any claims against the United States.
Approved November 23, 1993

The Apology for Slavery: Just Get Over It! Really?
by
Patricia M. Kirtley

An apology for an obvious wrong is often immediate, personal, and quickly forgotten. For the United States of America one affront lasted over 300 years and divided this country in a civil war. Some seek to excuse the introduction of slavery on the emerging American continent by elucidating its existence in ancient times and its presence in sacred texts including the Bible. Others cite the economic necessity for labor in the burgeoning new nation. Though both of these arguments are plausible, opponents claim outright ownership of human beings is immoral regardless of the circumstances. The apology for slavery by the United States constitutes a meaningful chapter in this ongoing debate. The United States House of Representatives issued the first apology in 2008. The United States Senate concurred one year later.

Roy Brooks (1999), University of San Diego Distinguished Law Professor, chronicled in *When Sorry Isn't Enough*, the first blacks to arrive in North America in 1619 initially enjoyed a measure of economic, as well as, social and political freedom. This freedom rapidly disappeared when individual colonies passed laws protecting slavery (p. 309). The treatment of millions of enslaved Africans was brutal, inhumane, and cruel. After capturing African slaves, traders separated families and sold them as animals or inanimate objects. By the dawn of the new American nation, the authors of independence proved to be enthusiastic but remarkably near-sighted. Indeed all men are created equal referred only to Caucasians.

One hundred years after the founding of the American nation, slavery was rampant. By the 1850s, Abolitionists in the Northern states argued vehemently for the end of slavery and the inhuman treatment of African slaves, while citizens of Southern states defended the right to slave labor to maintain their agricultural economy based on cotton, tobacco, and sugar. In 1857, US Supreme Court Chief Justice Robert Brooke Taney unfortunately ruled, in *Dred Scott v. Sandford*(1857), "blacks were regarded as beings of an inferior order . . . unfit to associate with the white race" and "had no right which the white man had to respect" (cited in Brooks, *When sorry,* 1999, p. 309).

The eventual result of these heated partisan debates was the American Civil War (1861-1865) that nearly destroyed the South and cost the new nation over 600,000 lives. Though the 13th Amendment to the United States Constitution abolished slavery in 1865 after the Civil War, African Americans soon saw justice compromised by Jim Crow laws that reinforced racism and the separation of African Americans from their rightful equality. These heinous post-Reconstruction laws mandated segregation on public transportation, in restrooms, restaurants, schools, and theaters. Finally, the Supreme Court ruled in *Brown v. Board of Education* (1954) that state laws requiring segregation of public schools were unconstitutional. *The Civil Rights Act of 1964* and *Voting Rights Act of 1965* abolished all remaining Jim Crow laws.

Steve Cohen (D-TN), with 120 co-sponsors, on 30 July 2008 introduced a resolution in the US House of Representatives to apologize for the institution of slavery and the Jim Crow laws that followed. In a building built with slave labor, Representative Cohen urged his colleagues to pass the resolution "because only a great nation can recognize and admit its mistakes and create a more perfect union" (House Resolution. 194, See appendix). Cohen'sresolutionrecognized the presence of slavery in the American colonies and the United States from 1619 through 1865 and concluded with a commitment to stop the occurrence of human rights violations in the future.

Senator Tom Harkin (D-IA) introduced a resolution apologizing for the enslavement and racial segregation of African Americans on 18 July 2009. One very important disclaimer concluded, "nothing in this resolution authorizes or supports any claim against the United States" (Senate Concurrent Resolution 26). Professor Kaimipono David Wenger (2009) stated in the *Connecticut Law Review,* "Unlike the House apology, the Senate apology contains additional limiting language, specifically stating that it cannot be used as a ground for monetary compensation" (p.1).

Several individual states passed their own apologies for slavery. Virginia was the first state to pass a resolution condemning slavery in February 2007 followed by Maryland, North Carolina, Alabama, New Jersey, and Florida. Verbal discussion on a slavery apology before and after the passage of the Senate's resolution was often passionate and verbose. Individual resistance to an apology for slavery in the American colonies and subsequent United States followed a remarkably consistent mantra.

Columnist Leonard Pitts (9 April, 1998), commented in his article, "Slavery Apology was Fitting and Proper" that, after President Bill Clinton's visit to Africa, columnist George Will, commentator Pat Buchanan, and former US House Majority Leader Tom Delay (R-TX) vehemently objected to Clinton's remarks, "European Americans received the fruits of the slave trade. And we were wrong in that" (p.1). The real invective came from columnist Robert Novak. On CNN's "Crossfire," he repeatedly referred to blacks as "you people" and railed that his ancestors lived in other countries at the time of slavery so no apology was necessary. He also noted the delegation of successful African Americans accompanying Clinton provided clear and convincing evidence that their success resulted from the slave trade. "If it hadn't been for slavery, they wouldn't even be in America, would they?" (cited in Pitts, 1998, p.1).

Olympia Meola and Robin Farmer (2007, February 4), wrote in their *Richmond Times Dispatch* (VA) article, "Local residents split over value of slavery apology," Virginia state legislator Frank D. Hargrove (R-Hanover) proposed his state celebrate Juneteenth, to commemorate the end of slavery on 19 June 1865. He opposed any apology for slavery because no one living today was involved in it. He said of slavery, "Our black citizens should get over it" (p. A-1).

Critic Camille Paglia (1999) claimed in her magazine column, "Who is really to blame for the historical scar of black slavery?" only offending parties could give apologies for their transgressions and her "people had nothing to do with African slave trade" (p. 353). She stated slavery existed worldwide, especially in Third World countries, and any American apology should include concurrent apologies from all cooperating nations of the West and Central Africa. She noted an apology was an "empty gesture" while the real need was to focus on the future and multiculturalism. She concluded, "The obsession with slavery—abolished here nearly a century and a half ago—is itself a form of enslavement" (p. 354).

For some the mere mention of monetary reparation was a sticking place to the endorsement of this apology, even though the joint resolution clearly included a disclaimer. Wenger (2009) stated, "the existence of numerous official apologies which give no legal right to compensation (most recently to Native Hawaiians) shows that an apology does not automatically grant the right to compensation" (p. 2). Reparation may not even be possible, but the imminently plausible suggestion of a federally funded and maintained national museum of slavery is a strong and practical opportunity. Brooks (2004) suggested in *Atonement and Forgiveness: A New Model for Black Reparations* building a slavery museum patterned on the Holocaust Museum in Washington, D.C. or the Simon Wiesenthal Center Museum in Los Angeles (p.157). He hoped, "For the vast majority of Americans, the museum will challenge their thinking and, it may be hoped, transform them" (p. 159).

Ramifications of slavery and subsequent Jim Crow laws continue to this day. Repetition of the glib comment African Americans should "Just get over it!" is insulting and degrading. Austina J. Hume, an African American resident of Richmond, Virginia stated she sees a "denial of responsibility" by people who say they had nothing to do with slavery but enjoy the benefits inherited from that system" (Meola and Farmer, 2007, p. A1). She comments both sides paid a huge price, denial is stressful, and African Americans want nothing more than for it to be over. "An apology would relieve white members of society of the weight of their psychological burden for the better of us all. If white people 'get over it,' it would be over" (Meola and Farmer, 2007, p. A1).

If America is to achieve progress in the 21st century, it must avoid the labyrinth of obfuscation and recommit to the 2009 apology passed as a joint Congressional Resolution. "Recognizing the injustice and abomination of slavery in America calls on all people of the United States to work toward eliminating racial prejudices, injustices, and discrimination from our society" (Senate Concurrent Resolution 26). This cannot remain an empty platitude. Only with recommitment to the principle all people are created equal and endowed with inalienable rights will the pursuit of happiness be possible.

Resources

Brooks, R. (2004). *Atonement and forgiveness: a new model for black reparations.* Berkeley CA: University of California Press.

Brooks, R. (Ed). (1999). *When sorry isn't enough.* New York: New York University.

Daniels, R. (1999). Redress achieved, 1983-1990. In Brooks, R. (Ed.) *When sorry isn't enough.*

Daniels, R. (1999). Relocation, redress, and the report. In Brooks, R. (Ed.) *When sorry isn't enough.*

House Resolution 194, July 29, 2008, Text apologizing for the enslavement and racial segregation of African-Americans. Retrieved from https://www.govtrack.us/congress/bills/110/hres194/text.

Meola, O. and Farmer, R. (2007, February 4). Local residents split over value of slavery apologies. *Richmond Times Dispatch* (VA), p. A-1.

Paglia, C. (1999). Who is really to blame for the historical scar of black slavery? In Brooks, R. (Ed.). (1999). *When sorry isn't enough*: pgs. 353-354.

Pitts, L. (1998, April 9). Slavery apology was
        fitting and proper. *The Baltimore Sun*, p.1.

Senate Concurrent Resolution 26. (2009, June
        18). 111th Cong. Retrieved from
        https://www.govtrack.us/congress/bills/1
        11/sconres26/text.

Wenger, K. D. (2009). Apology lite: truths,
        doubts, and reconciliations in the Senate's
        guarded apology for slavery. *Connecticut
        Law Review*: pgs. 1-7.

C. Appendix for Slavery

C.1. House Resolution 194, (July 29, 2008).Text apologizing for the enslavement and racial segregation of African-Americans. Retrieved from https://www.govtrack.us/congress/bills/110/hres194/text

Whereas millions of Africans and their descendants were enslaved in the United States and the 13 American colonies from 1619 through 1865;

Whereas slavery in America resembled no other form of involuntary servitude known in history, as Africans were captured and sold at auction like inanimate objects or animals;

Whereas Africans forced into slavery were brutalized, humiliated, dehumanized, and subjected to the indignity of being stripped of their names and heritage;

Whereas enslaved families were torn apart after having been sold separately from one another;

Whereas the system of slavery and the visceral racism against persons of African descent upon which it depended became entrenched in the Nation's social fabric;

Whereas slavery was not officially abolished until the passage of the 13th Amendment to the United States Constitution in 1865 after the end of the Civil War;

Whereas after emancipation from 246 years of slavery, African-Americans soon saw the fleeting political, social, and economic gains they made during Reconstruction eviscerated by virulent racism, lynchings, disenfranchisement, Black Codes, and racial segregation laws that imposed a rigid system of officially sanctioned racial segregation in virtually all areas of life;

Whereas the system of de jure racial segregation known as "Jim Crow," which arose in certain parts of the Nation following the Civil War to create separate and unequal societies for whites and African-Americans, was a direct result of the racism against persons of African descent engendered by slavery;

Whereas a century after the official end of slavery in America, Federal action was required during the 1960s to eliminate the dejure and defacto system of Jim Crow throughout parts of the Nation, though its vestiges still linger to this day;

Whereas African-Americans continue to suffer from the complex interplay between slavery and Jim Crow—long after both systems were formally abolished—through enormous damage and loss, both tangible and intangible, including the loss of human dignity, the frustration of careers and professional lives, and the long-term loss of income and opportunity;

Whereas the story of the enslavement and de jure segregation of African-Americans and the dehumanizing atrocities committed against them should not be purged from or minimized in the telling of American history;

Whereas on July 8, 2003, during a trip to Goree Island, Senegal, a former slave port, President George W. Bush acknowledged slavery's continuing legacy in American life and the need to confront that legacy when he stated that slavery "was . . . one of the greatest crimes of history . . . The racial bigotry fed by slavery did not end with slavery or with segregation. And many of the issues that still trouble America have roots in the bitter experience of other times. But however long the journey, our destiny is set: liberty and justice for all.";

Whereas President Bill Clinton also acknowledged the deep-seated problems caused by the continuing legacy of racism against African-Americans that began with slavery when he initiated a national dialogue about race;

Whereas a genuine apology is an important and necessary first step in the process of racial reconciliation;

Whereas an apology for centuries of brutal dehumanization and injustices cannot erase the past, but confession of the wrongs committed can speed racial healing and reconciliation and help Americans confront the ghosts of their past;

Whereas the legislature of the Commonwealth of Virginia has recently taken the lead in adopting a resolution officially expressing appropriate remorse for slavery and other State legislatures have adopted or are considering similar resolutions; and

Whereas it is important for this country, which legally recognized slavery through its Constitution and its laws, to make a formal apology for slavery and for its successor, Jim Crow, so that it can move forward and seek reconciliation, justice, and harmony for all of its citizens: Now, therefore, be it

That the House of Representatives—

(1) acknowledges that slavery is incompatible with the basic founding principles recognized in the Declaration of

Independence that all men are created equal;

(2) acknowledges the fundamental injustice, cruelty, brutality, and inhumanity of slavery and Jim Crow;

(3) apologizes to African Americans on behalf of the people of the United States, for the wrongs committed against them and their ancestors who suffered under slavery and Jim Crow; and

(4) expresses its commitment to rectify the lingering consequences of the misdeeds committed against African Americans under slavery and Jim Crow and to stop the occurrence of human rights violations in the future.

Clerk.

C.2. Senate Concurrent Resolution 26.

(2009, June 18). 111th Congress.Retrieved from https://www.congress.gov/bill/111th-congress/senate-concurrent-resolution/26/text

Apologizing for the enslavement and racial segregation of African-Americans.

Whereas during the history of the Nation, the United States has grown into a symbol of democracy and freedom around the world;

Whereas the legacy of African-Americans is interwoven with the very fabric of the democracy and freedom of the United States;

Whereas millions of Africans and their descendants were enslaved in the United States and the 13 American colonies from 1619 through 1865;

Whereas Africans forced into slavery were brutalized, humiliated, dehumanized, and subjected to the indignity of being stripped of their names and heritage;

Whereas many enslaved families were torn apart after family members were sold separately;

Whereas the system of slavery and the visceral racism against people of African descent upon which it depended became enmeshed in the social fabric of the United States;

Whereas slavery was not officially abolished until the ratification of the 13th amendment to the Constitution of the United States in 1865, after the end of the Civil War;

Whereas after emancipation from 246 years of slavery, African-Americans soon saw the fleeting political, social, and economic gains they made during Reconstruction eviscerated by virulent racism, lynchings, disenfranchisement, Black Codes, and racial segregation laws that imposed a rigid system of officially sanctioned racial segregation in virtually all areas of life;

Whereas the system of de jure racial segregation known as "Jim Crow", which arose in certain parts of the United States after the Civil War to create separate and unequal societies for Whites and African-Americans, was a direct result of the racism against people of African descent that was engendered by slavery;

Whereas the system of Jim Crow laws officially existed until the 1960s—a century after the official end of slavery in the United States—until Congress took action to end it, but the vestiges of Jim Crow continue to this day;

Whereas African-Americans continue to suffer from the consequences of slavery and Jim Crow laws—long after both systems were formally abolished—through enormous damage and loss, both tangible and intangible, including the loss of human dignity and liberty;

Whereas the story of the enslavement and de jure segregation of African-Americans and the dehumanizing atrocities committed against them should not be purged from or minimized in the telling of the history of the United States;

Whereas those African-Americans who suffered under slavery and Jim Crow laws, and their descendants, exemplify the strength of the human character and provide a model of courage, commitment, and perseverance;

Whereas on July 8, 2003, during a trip to Goree Island, Senegal, a former slave port, President George W. Bush acknowledged the continuing legacy of slavery in life in the United States and the need to confront that legacy, when he stated that slavery "was . . . one of the greatest crimes of history . . . The racial bigotry fed by slavery did not end with slavery or with segregation. And many of the issues that still trouble America have roots in the bitter experience of other times. But however long the journey, our destiny is set: liberty and justice for all.";

Whereas President Bill Clinton also acknowledged the deep-seated problems caused by the continuing legacy of racism against African-Americans that began with slavery, when he initiated a national dialogue about race;

Whereas an apology for centuries of brutal dehumanization and injustices cannot erase the past, but confession of the wrongs committed and a formal apology to African-Americans will help bind the wounds of the Nation that are rooted in slavery and can speed racial healing and reconciliation and help the people of the United States understand the past and honor the history of all people of the United States;

Whereas the legislatures of the Commonwealth of Virginia and the States of Alabama, Florida, Maryland, and North Carolina have taken the lead in adopting resolutions officially expressing appropriate remorse for slavery, and other State legislatures are considering similar resolutions; and

Whereas it is important for the people of the United States, who legally recognized slavery through the Constitution and the laws of the United States, to make a formal apology for slavery and for its successor, Jim Crow, so they can move forward and seek reconciliation, justice, and harmony for all people of the United States: Now, therefore, be it

That the sense of the Congress is the following:

(1) Apology for the enslavement and segregation of African-Americans

The Congress—

(A) acknowledges the fundamental injustice, cruelty, brutality, and inhumanity of slavery and Jim Crow laws;

(B) apologizes to African-Americans on behalf of the people of the United States, for the wrongs committed against them and their ancestors who suffered under slavery and Jim Crow laws; and

(C) expresses its recommitment to the principle that all people are created equal and endowed with inalienable rights to life, liberty, and the pursuit of happiness, and calls on all people of the United States to work toward eliminating racial prejudices, injustices, and discrimination from our society.

(2) Disclaimer

Nothing in this resolution—

(A) authorizes or supports any claim against the United States; or

(B) serves as a settlement of any claim against the United States.

Passed the Senate June 18, 2009.

NANCY ERICKSON,

Secretary

Congress Apologizes to Native Americans?
by
William R. Curtis

In 2009 the United States Congress and President Obama "apologized" to Native American nations for violence, mistreatment, and neglect inflicted during the past 400 years. The underlying historical causes of this odious treatment were greed and racism. The United States government broke at least 371 treaties ratified between Native American nations, beginning in 1778 when the Delaware nation ceded their land to the federal government. Congress has plenary power over Native American affairs. This means the Legislative branch has the ultimate right to pass legislation governing Native Americans, even when legislation conflicts with or abrogates Indian treaties. When the Pilgrims landed at Plymouth Rock, Native Americans controlled all of the United States' eventual land mass; today, the 358 federally recognized Indian reservations comprise barely two percent of American soil (Egan, 2000).

In 1824 Congress created the Bureau of Indian Affairs, an agency within the War Department designed to work closely with the United States Army to enforce federal government policies. At times the federal government recognized Native American nations as self-governing, independent political communities with different cultures. At other times the government attempted to force Native Americans to assimilate into the White culture (Haug, 2015, p. 1). By the 1850s westward expansion into Native American occupied territory west of the Mississippi River greatly influenced federal policy.

The Indian Removal Act of 1830 established the precedent for federal government relocation—by force if necessary—of Native Americans to reservations in the Oklahoma Territory in response to demands of White settlers and gold miners. The President could grant lands west of the Mississippi River to Native American nations that agreed to abandon their homelands. Incentives to relocate to the new reservations included financial and material assistance. The federal government guaranteed the Native Americans would live on these reservations under the protection of the United States government forever (Indian Removal Act 1830).

For the next 44 years the federal government focused on moving Native Americans to designated reservations. During the displacement, many indigenous people suffered and perished. The infamous Trail of Tears, the Sand Creek Massacre in 1864 and the Wounded Knee Massacre in 1890, are examples of the treatment of Native Americans during this period of American history.

President Andrew Jackson from Tennessee was a forceful proponent of Indian removal. He pushed the Indian Removal Act through both houses of Congress (Haug, 2015, p. 1). Jackson believed Native Americans were children who needed the guidance of wise White men. The President's beliefs reflected the paternalistic, patronizing attitude current at that time. Removal would save the Native Americans from the depredations of White men. While some

Native American nations, such as the Choctaws in 1830 and the Chickasaws in 1832, voluntarily agreed to relocate, the Seminoles, Creeks, and Cherokees resisted.

A small faction of the Cherokee tribe agreed to sign a removal agreement in 1833. The leaders of this group were not the recognized leaders of the Cherokee nation, and over 15,000 Cherokees, led by Chief John Ross, signed a petition in protest. The Supreme Court ignored their demands and ratified the treaty in 1836. The government gave the Cherokee two years to immigrate. Any remaining tribal members, at the end of that time, faced forcible removal. The United States government sent in 7,000 troops who drove the Native Americans into stockades at bayonet point. The soldiers did not allow tribal members to gather their belongings and, as the Cherokee left, Whites looted their homes and seized their lands (Indian Removal Act, 1830).

Thus began the Trail of Tears march in which at least 4,000 of the 16,543 relocated Cherokee died of cold, hunger, and disease on their way to the western lands. By 1837 the United States government removed 46,000 Native Americans from their homelands in the southeastern states, thereby opening 25 million acres for settlement. The Seminole tribe in Florida, which resisted the removal, fought three wars against the United States and never signed a peace treaty with the federal government.

The first government apology came from Kevin Gover, a Pawnee and head of the Bureau of Indian Affairs (BIA) during the Clinton administration. Gover apologized for his agency's "legacy of racism and inhumanity" on the 175th anniversary of the BIA on September 8, 2000. He stated clearly his remarks applied only to the BIA and he did not presume to speak for the "nation's elected leaders" (Gover, 2000). An audience of 300 tribal leaders, BIA officials, and federal officials cheered when a teary-eyed Gover finished his speech. Some Native American leaders praised Gover's remarks. Others pointed out the irony of a Native American apologizing to Native Americans and the limited nature of his apology. Eugene Johnson (Siletz) termed the apology "truly offensive" and Jim Craven (Blackfoot) called it an "obscene cover-up" (Kelly, 2000, para. 9).

The Senate of the United States finally apologized to Native Americans in 2009. (McKinnon). Senators Sam Brownback (R-KS) and Byron Dorgan (D-ND) drafted an apology and led the campaign for its acceptance. Brownback proposed a preamble that provided historical context to the measure. The Senator from Kansas mentioned Native Americans often provided help to settlers. He detailed multiple massacres of Indian women and children, the harsh cruelty of Trail of Tears, the Sand Creek Massacre, the Battle of Wounded Knee, the theft of tribal lands and resources, the breaking of multiple treaties, and the forcible removal of Indian children from their homes to attend boarding schools many miles from their reservations. The Senate did not include this preamble in the final draft of the measure.

The Senate passed the resolution apologizing for the breaking of covenants, violence, maltreatment, and neglect of Native Americans (Senate Concurrent Resolution 26,

2009). The resolution commended native peoples for their stewardship of the land. The resolution expressed hope that the government could move toward reconciliation and build positive relationships with Native Americans. It urged the President of the United States to publicly acknowledge these injustices and commended states that had done so. The resolution did not support reparations or claims against the government.

Congress buried this resolution in the 2010 Defense Appropriations Act among appropriations for billions of dollars for weapons and other items (H.R. 3326, Public Law No. 111-118). President Obama signed the act into law on Saturday, December 19, 2009. He did so privately, with no press in attendance. The lack of openness on the part of the President and Congress convinced many Native Americans that these hidden apologies were half-hearted and insincere.

President Obama previously noted the federal government violated treaties with tribes and perpetrated injustices against them at a White House tribal nations conference. Conference members urged the President to publicly acknowledge the wrongs of the United States against Indian tribes in order to bring healing to this land. Obama failed to honor their request by signing the document in private. Robert T. Coulter, executive director of the Indian Law Resource Center, considered this as another example of the "overwhelming silence" regarding the resolution (as cited in Capriccioso, 2010, para. 19).

Public apologies have a long history of healing transgressions against humanity. The international human rights framework considers public admissions of responsibility by state officials a significant part of conflict resolution and reconciliation. The operative word here is "public." Senator Brownback read the resolution at the Congressional cemetery on May 20, 2010. Present were representatives from the Cherokee, Choctaw, Muscogee (Creek), Sisseton Wahpeton Oyate, and Pawnee nations.

The United States government made several feeble attempts to apologize to Native Americans. Dennis Gringold, a Native American rights attorney, commented, "It is not whether you apologize for doing something terrible, it's whether you do something about it. If you don't do anything, it probably is insulting" (Florio, 2015, p. 2). A few paragraphs in the 2009 defense-spending bill are a meager beginning. Hundreds of years of maltreatment and abuse of America's indigenous people demands more. Native Americans deserve a complete, equitable, and public apology.

Resources

Capriccioso, R. (2010, January 13). A sorry, saga: Obama signs Native American apology resolution, fails to draw attention to it. *Indian Law Center*. Retrieved from http://www.indianlaw.org/node/529.

Defense Appropriations Bill (2009).Public Law 111-118, December 19, 2009, 111th Congress. Sec. 8113. (a).Retrieved from http://. copywright.gov/legislation/pl111-118.pdf.

Egan, T. (2000). The nation: Mending a trail of broken treaties.*New York Times*. Retrieved from http://www.nytimes.com/2000/06/25/weekinreview/the-nation.

Florio, G. (2015). Indians still await formal apology.*Missoulian Newspaper*. Retrieved from http://missoulian.com/news/local/indians-still-await-formal-apology/article.

Gover, K. (2000). Gover BIA speech. *YouTube*. Retrieved from https://www.youtube.

Haug, C. (2015). *Victoriana Magazine*. (2015). Native American tribes & US government. Retrieved from http://www.victoriana.com/history/nativeamericans.

Indian Removal Act. (1830, May 28). Primary
Documents in American History. Library
of Congress. Retrieved from loc.gov.

Kelly, M. (2007). Indian affairs head makes
apology. *Associated Press.* Retrieved from
http//chs.umn.edu.

McKinnon, J. D. (2009). US offers an official
apology to Native Americans. *Wall Street
Journal.* Retrieved from
http://blogs.wsj.com.

Senate Joint Resolution 14 (2009). Retrieved
from
http://thomas.loc.gov/chi-bin
/query/z?c111:S.J.RES.14:

D. Appendix for Native Americans

D.1. Excerpt from Defense Appropriations Bill (2009). Public Law 111-118, December 19, 2009, 111th Congress. Sec. 8113. (a). Retrieved from http://www.copywright.gov/legislation/pl111-118.pdf.

Acknowledgment and Apology - The United States, acting through Congress

(1) recognizes the special legal and political relationship Indian tribes have with the United States and the solemn covenant with the land we share;

(2) commends and honors Native Peoples for the thousands of years that they have stewarded and protected this land;

(3) recognizes that there have been years of official depredations, ill-conceived policies, and the breaking of covenants by the Federal Government regarding Indian tribes;

(4) apologizes on behalf of the people of the United States to all Native Peoples for the many instances of violence, mal- treatment, and neglect inflicted on Native Peoples by citizens of the United States;

(5) expresses its regret for the ramifications of former wrongs and its commitment to build on the positive relation- ships of the past and present to move toward a brighter future where all the people of this land live reconciled as brothers and sisters, and harmoniously steward and protect this land together;

(6) urges the President to acknowledge the wrongs of the United States against Indian tribes in the history of the United States in order to bring healing to this land; and

(7) commends the State governments that have begun reconciliation efforts with recognized Indian tribes located in their boundaries and encourages all State governments similarly to work toward reconciling relationships with Indian tribes within their boundaries.

(b) DISCLAIMER. —Nothing in this section—
(1) authorizes or supports any claim against the United States; or

(2) serves as a settlement of any claim against the United States.

D.2. Joint Resolution 14 (2014). Retrieved from http://thomas.loc.gov/chi-bin /query/z?c111:S.J.RES.14:

To acknowledge a long history of official depredations and ill-conceived policies by the Federal Government regarding Indian tribes and offer an apology to all Native Peoples on behalf.

Whereas the ancestors of today's Native Peoples inhabited the land of the present-day United States since time immemorial and for thousands of years before the arrival of people of European descent;

Whereas for millennia, Native Peoples have honored, protected, and stewarded this land we cherish;

Whereas Native Peoples are spiritual

people with a deep and abiding belief in the Creator, and for millennia Native Peoples have maintained a powerful spiritual connection to this land, as evidenced by their customs and legends;

Whereas the arrival of Europeans in North America opened a new chapter in the history of Native Peoples;

Whereas while establishment of permanent European settlements in North America did stir conflict with nearby Indian tribes, peaceful and mutually beneficial interactions also took place;

Whereas the foundational English settlements in Jamestown, Virginia, and Plymouth, Massachusetts, owed their survival in large measure to the compassion and aid of Native Peoples in the vicinities of the settlements;

Whereas in the infancy of the United States, the founders of the Republic expressed their desire for a just relationship with the Indian tribes, as evidenced by the Northwest Ordinance enacted by Congress in 1787, which begins with the phrase, `The utmost good faith shall always be observed toward the Indians';

Whereas Indian tribes provided great assistance to the fledgling Republic as it strengthened and grew, including invaluable help to Meriwether Lewis and William Clark on their epic journey from St. Louis, Missouri, to the Pacific Coast;

Whereas Native Peoples and non-Native settlers engaged in numerous armed conflicts in which unfortunately, both took innocent lives, including those of women and children;

Whereas the Federal Government violated many of the treaties ratified by Congress and other diplomatic agreements with Indian tribes;

Whereas the United States forced Indian tribes and their citizens to move away from their traditional homelands and onto federally established and controlled reservations, in accordance with such Acts as the Act of May 28, 1830 (4 Stat. 411, chapter 148) (commonly known as the `Indian Removal Act');

Whereas many Native Peoples suffered and perished--

(1) during the execution of the official Federal Government policy of forced removal, including the infamous Trail of Tears and Long Walk;

(2) during bloody armed confrontations and massacres, such as the Sand Creek Massacre in 1864 and the Wounded Knee Massacre in 1890; and

(3) on numerous Indian reservations;

Whereas the Federal Government condemned the traditions, beliefs, and customs of Native Peoples and endeavored to assimilate them by such policies as the redistribution of land under the Act of February 8, 1887 (25 U.S.C. 331; 24 Stat. 388, chapter 119) (commonly known as the `General Allotment Act'), and the forcible removal of Native children from their families to faraway boarding schools where their Native practices and languages were degraded and forbidden;

Whereas officials of the Federal Government and private United States citizens harmed Native Peoples by the unlawful acquisition of recognized tribal land and the theft of tribal resources and assets from recognized tribal land;

Whereas the policies of the Federal

Government toward Indian tribes and the breaking of covenants with Indian tribes have contributed to the severe social ills and economic troubles in many Native communities today;

Whereas despite the wrongs committed against Native Peoples by the United States, Native Peoples have remained committed to the protection of this great land, as evidenced by the fact that, on a per capita basis, more Native Peoples have served in the United States Armed Forces and placed themselves in harm's way in defense of the United States in every major military conflict than any other ethnic group;

Whereas Indian tribes have actively influenced the public life of the United States by continued cooperation with Congress and the Department of the Interior, through the involvement of Native individuals in official Federal Government positions, and by leadership of their own sovereign Indian tribes;

Whereas Indian tribes are resilient and determined to preserve, develop, and transmit to future generations their unique cultural identities;

Whereas the National Museum of the American Indian was established within the Smithsonian Institution as a living memorial to Native Peoples and their traditions; and

Whereas Native Peoples are endowed by their Creator with certain unalienable rights, and among those are life, liberty, and the pursuit of happiness: Now, therefore, be it

Resolved by the Senate and House of Representatives of the United States of America in Congress assembled,

Section 1. Resolution of Apology to Native Peoples of the United States. SECTION 1.

(a) Acknowledgment and Apology- The United States, acting through Congress—

(1) recognizes the special legal and political relationship Indian tribes have with the United States and the solemn covenant with the land we share;

(2) commends and honors Native Peoples for the thousands of years that they have stewarded and protected this land;

(3) recognizes that there have been years of official depredations, ill-conceived policies, and the breaking of covenants by the Federal Government regarding Indian tribes;

(4) apologizes on behalf of the people of the United States to all Native Peoples for the many instances of violence, maltreatment, and neglect inflicted on Native Peoples by citizens of the United States;

(5) expresses its regret for the ramifications of former wrongs and its commitment to build on the positive relationships of the past and present to move toward a brighter future where all the people of this land live reconciled as brothers and sisters, and harmoniously steward and protect this land together;

(6) urges the President to acknowledge the wrongs of the United States against Indian tribes in the history of the United States in order to bring healing to this land; and

(7) commends the State governments that have begun reconciliation efforts with recognized Indian tribes located in their boundaries and encourages all State governments similarly to

work toward reconciling relationships with Indian tribes within their boundaries.

(b) Disclaimer- Nothing in this Joint Resolution—

(1) authorizes or supports any claim against the United States; or

(2) serves as a settlement of any claim against the United States.

The United States Congress Apologizes to the Chinese
by
Terry L. Lovelace

Chink! Coolie! Slant-eye! Barbarian! Yellow peril! Heathen! Rat eater! First came shocking racial epithets, then blatant discriminatory laws led to physical violence, exclusion, murder, and finally--an apology. It is time to face the truth. Again, the underlying historical causes of the violence, mistreatment, and neglect of Chinese in America were greed and racism. Discrimination against all people of color began early. In 1790 Congress passed the Naturalization Act that stated only free White persons could become American citizens.

The first period of Chinese immigration began shortly after the California Gold Rush and ended abruptly with the passage of the Chinese Exclusion Act of 1882. During this period, thousands of young male Chinese peasants left their rural villages to become laborers in the American West. According to Representative Judy Chu (D-CA), "their blood, sweat, and tears built the first transcontinental railroad, connecting the people of our nation. They opened our mines, constructed the levies, and became the backbone of farm production" (cited in Basu, 2012, p. 1).

On October 6, 2011, Congress apologized to Chinese-Americans for cruel laws adopted so many years ago. Senator Diane Feinstein (D-CA), sponsor of the bill, stated "I hope this resolution will serve to enlighten those who may not be aware of this regrettable chapter in our history, and bring closure to the families whose loved ones lived through this difficult time" (cited in Basu, 2012, p.1).

Chinese men came to California in the 1840's to escape poverty, famine, and overpopulation. After the discovery of gold in 1848, unscrupulous ship owners distributed recruiting pamphlets to lure Asian men, eager to make their fortune mining California's Gam Saan (Gold Mountain). The state of California levied a Foreign Miners Tax of $20/month on the new workers. California levied taxes that applied only to Chinese. They forced Chinese fishermen to purchase a special fishing license and pay a "police tax," ostensibly to pay law enforcement costs associated with the Chinese community. The real reason for these discriminatory taxes was to raise revenue for the state, up to 50 percent of California state revenue (Asian American Artistry, 2010).

Between 1850 and 1882, 322,000 Chinese came to the United States, most of them from southern provinces of China. This massive immigration generated such panic in California that the state banned further immigration of Chinese, passed laws preventing Chinese-Americans from testifying against Whites, and excluded Chinese children from attending public schools.

TheCentral Pacific Railroad Company used Chinese laborers almost exclusively (90%) to build the transcontinental railroad in the west (1864-1869). The Chinese provided cheap labor. These workers could not become citizens and had no opportunity for education, housing, or jobs. In 1867 Chinese railway laborers staged a nonviolent two-week strike for better working conditions. The railroad subsequently cut off the workers' rations and forced them back to work. The strike was broken. The railroad companies, despite their claim that beatings and whippings were necessary to motivate and discipline their 5,000 to 7,000 Chinese workers, agreed to stop these brutal punishments (Cohen, 2010, p. 1).

Due to the need for Chinese labor, American diplomats negotiated the Burlingame-Seward Treaty (1868) that recognized the rights of Chinese citizens to immigrate to the United States and promised reciprocal privileges of residence, school, and travel. The treaty granted Secretary of State William Seward the right to preempt California laws discriminating against Chinese citizens (Cohen, 2010). Federal courts extended the right of due process included in the Fourteenth Amendment (1868) and the enforcement powers granted by the Civil Rights Act (1870) to allow Chinese nationals to testify in court and forbidding the imposition of discriminatory penalties, taxes, and licenses. However, Congress retained the law barring Asian aliens from citizenship.

In 1870 the American Union Labor group supported anti-Chinese ordinances in San Francisco. To prevent multiple Chinese from sharing housing in the urban area, the city passed a Cubic Air ordinance requiring 500 square feet for every adult in a dwelling. Congress also passed a law that limited the number of Chinese passengers on any ship coming to the United States; however, President Rutherford Hayes vetoed this bill on the grounds it was inconsistent with US–China treaty commitments.

An economic depression hit the United States in the 1870s after the Civil War, and American workers lost their jobs. Anti-Chinese sentiment increased enormously and the Chinese laborers became scapegoats. A scarcity of gold increased competition and exacerbated animosity between White and Chinese miners. Forced out of mining and other occupations, many Chinese settled in densely populated ghettos in cities like San Francisco where they worked in restaurants and laundries.

By 1879 Californians were so antagonistic toward the Chinese immigrants that the wording of the second constitution in California included verbiage preventing municipalities and corporations from employing Chinese. The California state legislature passed a law requiring incorporated towns and cities to move all Chinese outside of city limits, but the United States circuit court declared the law unconstitutional. Shipping companies smuggled thousands of Chinese women through San Francisco's immigrant station and sold them into slavery. Local newspapers printed arrival information. In 1882, California passed a law against the importation of Chinese, Japanese, and "Mongolian" women for prostitution. The 1870 California census listed 61 percent (2,157) of the 3,536 Chinese women immigrants as prostitutes (Asian Pacific, 2010, p. 1).

In 1882 Congress passed the Chinese Exclusion Act, the only federal law ever enacted to deny immigration based exclusively on race or nationality. This law set a precedent for racist foreign and national policy. It led to broad exclusion laws and fostered an environment of racism in this country (Lew, 2014). This act was in effect for 61 years. It banned Chinese immigration to the United States and denied citizenship to Chinese people already living in the United States. It cruelly prevented thousands of Chinese men living in the United States from reuniting with the wives and children they left behind in China.

Passage of these laws intensified bigotry and led to mob violence in several cities. Anti-Chinese riots broke out in Seattle in 1886, and local authorities evicted the Chinese. Nearby Tacoma had the largest population of Chinese in Washington State (10%). A leading newspaper hoped Tacoma would soon be a town without a Chinaman (Asian Pacific, 2010). Mobs shouting racial epithets collected the Chinese and forced them onto a train bound for Portland.

The same year, the Knights of Labor, an early labor union, organized anti-Chinese demonstrations and riots in Portland, Oregon. Protesters smashed windows in Chinese shops and threatened violence if the Chinese did not leave the city. Some White business leaders resisted the Knights and quelled the anti-Chinese violence. Many Chinese fled, returning to China or moving to the eastern half of the United States. In 1887, a gang of horse thieves and ranch hands killed 31 Chinese miners on the Snake River in Oregon (Margolis, 2011).

The Supreme Court ruled the power of Congress over immigration was absolute. The first case to contest this decision was *Chae Chan Ping v. United States*. It involved a Chinese resident laborer in San Francisco. He obtained a reentry certificate before visiting China. Ping found on his return that an 1888 amendment retroactively voided his certificate. Immigration authorities detained him aboard ship in San Francisco Bay. The majority opinion stated the refusal of entry was legal and exclusion of Chinese laborers preserved American civilization and way of life (Chodorow, 2012). Congress passed the Geary Act (1892) requiring Chinese legally residing in the United States to carry a certificate of residence at all times and extended the Exclusion Act.

Racial prejudice translated into panic in 1899 when the bubonic plague broke out in Hawaii. Public officials in San Francisco followed the examples of their peers in Honolulu, closing Chinese businesses, mandating inoculations, placing the Chinese under quarantine, and cordoning off Chinatown with a nine-foot-tall fence—a quarantine later ruled unconstitutional by a federal court. The combined efforts of the ethnic San Francisco Chinese community, their lawyers, and China's ambassador to the United States saved the community from complete destruction.

Congress repealed the Chinese Exclusion Act in 1943 and replaced it with the Magnuson Act after China became an American ally against Japan in World War II (Basu, 2012, p. 1). The Magnuson Act allowed admission of 105 Chinese immigrants to America per year. The Walter-McCarran Act (1952) reformed the laws governing immigration to the United States. Overriding a veto by President Harry S. Truman, Congress established a system that favored immigration from Northern and Western Europe through quotas based on the 1920 census.

The United States finally allowed significant Chinese immigration after the passage of the Immigration and Nationality Act of 1965.

Three government entities eventually offered apologies to Chinese immigrants. On October 6, 2011, the Senate unanimously approved a resolution sponsored by Diane Feinstein (D-CA) apologizing for the nation's discriminatory laws that targeted Chinese immigrants. Senator Scott Brown (R-MA) co-sponsored the bill. He said it was "important that we recognize the wrongs that were committed so many years ago" (Margolis, 2011, p. 2). Senator Marco Rubio (R-FL) co-sponsored the bill. Members of the Chinese and Asian American communities including the Chinese American Citizens Alliance, the Japanese American Citizens League, and the American Jewish Committee lobbied for this apology.

On June 19, 2012, Rep. Judy Chu, (D-CA), the first Chinese-American woman elected to Congress, sponsored House Resolution 683 expressing regret for the passage of the Chinese Exclusion Act. Chu noted, "Today is historic" (Basu, 2012, p. 1). This apology was deeply personal as her grandfather experienced firsthand the prejudice generated by this act. On May 17, 2014, the State of California apologized for enacting discriminatory laws aimed at the Chinese and acknowledged their contributions to the state (SJR recognizes, 2010).

The Chinese Exclusion Act devastated the Chinese-American community and reinforced negative stereotypes. Senator Feinstein (2010) noted in a press release, "Despite these hardships, Chinese immigrants persevered, and they continued to make invaluable contributions to the development and success of our country" (p. 1). Congress issuing an apology on behalf of the American people for the Chinese Exclusion Act is appropriate. Representative Chu concurred, "The Senate did its part to right history" (Basu, 2012, p. 1). This apology informed Americans about a dreadful and unfortunate chapter in our national history. As a people, we need to take responsibility, admit our faults, and express heartfelt repentance for the wrongs done to Chinese-Americans who helped build this nation. In this lies strength and unity.

Resources

Asian Pacific American historical timeline details *(1875 to 1899):* our victories, obstaclesand leaders. (2010). *Asian Artistry.* Retrieved from http://us_asian.tripod.com.

Basu, M. (2012). In a rare apology, House regrets exclusionary laws targeting Chinese.*CNN blogs.* Retrieved from http://inamerica.blogs.cnn.com.

Chodorow. G. (2012). (2012). Congress has apologized for the Chinese Exclusion Act of 1882. *U.S. & China Visa Law Blog.* Retrieved from http://lawandborder.com.

Cohen, W. I. (2010). *America's response to China: A history of Sino-American relations (5th Ed.).* New York: Columbia University Press.

Feinstein, D. (2011, May 26). Feinstein resolution expresses regret for discriminatory laws against Chinese immigrants. *Feinstein Website.* Retrieved from feinstein.senate. gov.

House Resolution 683, June 18, 2012. Retrieved from www.govtrack.us/congress/bills/112/hres 683/text.

Lew, A. (2014). *Bill analysis: SJR 23.* Retrieved from http://www.leginfo.ca.gov/pub/13-14/bill/sen/sb_0001-

050/sjr_23_cfa_20140808_120124_asm
_comm.html.

Margolis, D. (2011). US Senate apologizes for
Chinese Exclusion Act.*People's World.*
Retrieved from http://peoplesworld.orgu-
s-senate-apologizes-for-chinese-
exclusion-act/.

SJR. (2014, May 7). State of California recognizes
history and contributions of Chinese
Americans. *Website Senator Bob Huff.*
Retrieved from
http://district29.cssrc.us/content/huff.

E. Appendix for Chinese Exclusion

E.1. House Resolution. 683, June 18, 2012.
Retrieved from www.govtrack.us/congress/bills/112/hres 683/text.

Whereas many Chinese came to the United States in the 19th and 20th centuries, as did people from other countries, in search of the opportunity to create a better life;

Whereas the United States ratified the Burlingame Treaty on October 19, 1868, which permitted the free movement of the Chinese people to, from, and within the United States and made China a "most favored nation";

Whereas in 1878, the House of Representatives passed a resolution requesting that President Rutherford B. Hayes renegotiate the Burlingame Treaty so Congress could limit Chinese immigration to the United States;

Whereas, on February 22, 1879, the House of Representatives passed the Fifteen Passenger Bill, which only permitted 15 Chinese passengers on any ship coming to the United States;

Whereas, on March 1, 1879, President Hayes vetoed the Fifteen Passenger Bill as being incompatible with the Burlingame Treaty;

Whereas, on May 9, 1881, the United States ratified the Angell Treaty, which allowed the United States to suspend, but not prohibit, immigration of Chinese laborers, declared that "Chinese laborers who are now in the United States shall be allowed to go and come of their own free will," and reaffirmed that Chinese persons possessed "all the rights, privileges, immunities, and exemptions which are accorded to the citizens and subjects of the most favored nation";

Whereas the House of Representatives passed legislation that adversely affected Chinese persons in the United States and limited their civil rights, including—

(1) on March 23, 1882, the first Chinese Exclusion bill, which excluded for 20 years skilled and unskilled Chinese laborers and expressly denied Chinese persons alone the right to be naturalized as American citizens, and which was opposed by President Chester A. Arthur as incompatible with the terms and spirit of the Angell Treaty;

(2) on April 17, 1882, intending to address President Arthur's concerns, the House passed a new Chinese Exclusion bill, which prohibited Chinese workers from entering the United States for 10 years instead of 20, required certain Chinese laborers already legally present in the United States who later wished to reenter the United States to obtain "certificates of return," and prohibited courts from naturalizing Chinese individuals;

(3) on May 3, 1884, an expansion of the Chinese Exclusion Act, which applied it to all persons of Chinese descent, "whether subjects of China or any other foreign power";

(4) on September 3, 1888, the Scott Act, which prohibited legal Chinese laborers from reentering the United States and cancelled all previously issued "certificates of return," and which was later determined by the Supreme Court to have abrogated the Angell Treaty; and

(5) on April 4, 1892, the Geary Act, which

reauthorized the Chinese Exclusion Act for another ten years, denied Chinese immigrants the right to be released on bail upon application for a writ of habeas corpus, and contrary to customary legal standards regarding the presumption of innocence, authorized the deportation of Chinese persons who could not produce a certificate of residence unless they could establish residence through the testimony of "at least one credible white witness";

Whereas in the 1894 Gresham-Yang Treaty, the Chinese government consented to a prohibition of Chinese immigration and the enforcement of the Geary Act in exchange for readmission to the United States of Chinese persons who were United States residents;

Whereas in 1898, the United States annexed Hawaii, took control of the Philippines, and excluded only the residents of Chinese ancestry of these territories from entering the United States mainland;

Whereas, on April 29, 1902, as the Geary Act was expiring, Congress indefinitely extended all laws regulating and restricting Chinese immigration and residence, to the extent consistent with Treaty commitments;

Whereas in 1904, after the Chinese government withdrew from the Gresham-Yang Treaty, Congress permanently extended, "without modification, limitation, or condition," the prohibition on Chinese naturalization and immigration;

Whereas these Federal statutes enshrined in law the exclusion of the Chinese from the democratic process and the promise of American freedom;

Whereas in an attempt to undermine the American-Chinese alliance during World War II, enemy forces used the Chinese exclusion legislation passed in Congress as evidence of anti-Chinese attitudes in the United States;

Whereas in 1943, in furtherance of American war objectives, at the urging of President Franklin D. Roosevelt, Congress repealed previously enacted legislation and permitted Chinese persons to become United States citizens;

Whereas Chinese-Americans continue to play a significant role in the success of the United States; and

Whereas the United States was founded on the principle that all persons are created equal: Now, therefore, be it

1. Acknowledgement

That the House of Representatives regrets the passage of legislation that adversely affected people of Chinese origin in the United States because of their ethnicity.

2. Disclaimer

Nothing in this resolution may be construed or relied on to authorize or support any claim, including but not limited to constitutionally based claims, claims for monetary compensation or claims for equitable relief against the United States or any other party, or serve as a settlement of any claim against the United States.

Clerk.

Conclusion

All five apologies analyzed in this paper helped correct violations of human rights. All had one thing in common – racism. There is no adequate definition of this ugly construct, but it flourishes when pseudo-scientific theories of racial superiority, prevail. These pernicious concepts erode people's belief in the equality of humans and their fundamental rights to liberty and justice. They open the door to cruelty and avarice. The apology and reparations, granted Japanese-Americans by Congress, established a model for subsequent apologies, an example never again fully realized. The President and/or Congress apologized, but not in consort. Congressional apologists adamantly stated that their expressions of sorrow did not constitute a legal claim for reparations. These apologies were necessary and beneficial, even in their flawed states. They initiated discussions of past injustices and encouraged remedial public policy. They allowed some a chance to voice their grievances and others the opportunity to examine their consciences. The United States will "get over it" when it looks at the past honestly, and recommits itself to the fundamental principle that all people are created equal.

About the Authors

Lem Londos Railsback earned a B.S. and an M.A. from Sul Ross State College, a Ph.D. from The University of Texas, an M.Ed. from the University of Texas at Brownsville, and an A.A. and an A.A.S. from Laredo Community College. He retired in 2009, after 50 years of teaching. Lem is a retired Navy Chief. He has visited 30 foreign nations, all 50 states in the United States, most of its major cities, and the District of Columbia. In retirement, he researches, writes, and presents at national professional conferences: he has 385 publications. Lem is a lifetime member of the American Association of University Professors and of the National Social Science Association. In 2015, N.S.S.A.honored Lem by naming him the Gail McClay Award N.S.S.A. 2014-2015 MEMBER OF THE YEAR. Helives in Laredo, Texas, six blocks from the Rio Grande, with his three pet dogs. Frequent visits from his girlfriend, former colleagues, and students keep him up to date on local matters.

William M. Kirtley lives in Medford, Oregon. He earned his MS. Ed from Southern Oregon University, MA in History from the University of Oregon, and a Doctor of Arts in Political Science from Idaho State University. He taught social science courses at the secondary level for 30 years and college level courses aboard deployed US Navy ships for Central Texas College for 19 years. Kirtley's work *Politics of Death* (2012)deals with the origins of the Death With Dignity movement. His co-authored paper, "Patriotism Is Not Enough: Nurse Edith Cavell" won the coveted National Social Science Association David Marx Award for NSSA National Journal Outstanding Article in 2015. He is the 2015-2017 president of the National Social Science Association.

Terry L. Lovelace earned her B.S. from Louisiana State University, M. Ed. from Auburn University, and Ph. D. in Reading Education from the University of Georgia. She recently retired after 40 years as an elementary education professor. Terry served as the past-president of the National Social Science Association (2013-2015). She co-authored an article, *Create a Digital World: Five Steps to Engage Students in Multi-Cultural Learning*. She resides on the Gulf Coast of Mississippi.

William (Bill) R. Curtis is a retired United States Army Chief Warrant Officer IV who served over 31 years in the military. Bill earned his BA in Art from Cameron University. Currently, he is a member of the Board of Directors of the National Social Science Association, happily mowing his acreage and supporting his wife's landscaping projects. He keeps the author team running smoothly with his wit, wisdom, and common sense.

Patricia M. Kirtley lives in Medford, Oregon. She earned a Masters of Fine Arts in Writing Children's Literature from Vermont College of Fine Arts. She also worked in a hospital laboratory for 40 years as a Medical Technologist, MT (ASCP). Her co-authored paper, "Patriotism Is Not Enough: Nurse Edith Cavell" won the coveted National Social Science Association David Marx Award for NSSA National Journal Outstanding Article in 2015. She serves on the Board of Directors of the National Social Science Association.

In 2015, this team of authors published the book, *Healthy Grieving: An Opportunity for Growth,* a collection of essays on grief.